Moments in Thought

Nikki LeRae

BookLeaf Publishing

India | USA | UK

Presentation by *BookLeaf Publishing*

Web: www.bookleafpub.com

E-mail: info@bookleafpub.com

ISBN: 9789358312959

First edition 2023

*Many, many thanks to James St. John, who
has been a steady source of encouragement
to "keep writing".*

Beautiful Spring Day

It's a beautiful, beautiful spring day
Bees buzz, dogs bark, birds tweet
in the distance, children play

The sun shines bright with warm rays
Flowers bloom and smell so sweet
It's a beautiful, beautiful spring day

Good to meet you, strangers say
In the park, friends will see you
In the distance, children play

Butterflies flutter about on display
Clouds form pictures that are neat
It's a beautiful, beautiful spring day

Moms call out with a lemonade tray
Hurry back to get your treat
In the distance, children play

Hurry outside, don't delay
The day is perfect, it is complete
It's a beautiful, beautiful spring day
In the distance, children play

Hot Summer Day

The fan blade spins around
Sharing it's cool breeze on my face
Offering a simple escape from the heat

It's a sweltering hot summer day
Sweat dripping from me without grace
The fan blade spins around

"We love the hot summer," others say
I beg the days to hurry and race
To bring Autumn, an escape from the heat

No energy to do more than just lay
And breathe at a steady pace
The fan blade spins around

The sun has rules it must obey
I settle into my favorite place
The fan blade spins around
Offering a simple escape from the heat

The Storm

Dark clouds, pouring down rain
I can hear the thunder clash
Hidden sun, it shines in vain

Cool wind spins the weather vane
Lightening fills the sky with a flash
Dark clouds, pouring down rain

Tree Branches bend, howling in pain
Puddles make a big splash
Hidden sun, it shines in vain

Hail fails, it looks like grain
I wonder how long this will last
Dark clouds, pouring down rain

The storm has taken the reign
It isn't ready to pass
Dark clouds, pouring down rain
Hidden sun, it shines in vain

Forever Love

His warm embrace is all I'll ever need
His tender touch, his passionate kisses
If I begin to stumble, he will lead
I won't fall, he never misses

I will always find solace in his arms
He brings me joy and fills me with laughter
He erases my worries and alarms
He is my happily ever after

Time serves only to strengthen our bond
Years have passed - his embrace is still warm
Love will remain with us while time absconds
Touches and kisses have become the norm

Age may have tempered some our passionate
ways
Our embraces will nurture the rest of our days

Ode to Yellowstone

A bounty of beauty is to be found in
Yellowstone
Bison roam the fields and forests, such mighty
beasts
While snow capped mountains create stunning
waterfalls
Steam rises in the air marking the many geysers
That contribute to the magestic scenes in it's
nature
As evening approaches the sky fills with a
sunset

Oranges, blues, pinks, and purples paint the
colorful sunset
In the sky after the day's adventures in
Yellowstone
All of these colors in the sky compliment the
park's protected nature
Elk, moose, bison, and more are just some of the
beasts
That make their homes in the forests near the
geysers
And next to the mountain streams and
waterfalls.

Log jams and giant boulders add beauty to the
waterfalls
Just like the setting sun brings a beautiful sunset
Many hot springs, deep and blue, are also
erupting geysers
There truly is no end to the awe and beauty of
Yellowstone
Grizzly mom and cubs are just a few more of the
beasts
Found in the mountain forests and fields in the
nature

Flowers are seen blooming throughout the
serene nature
They are in the fields, the mountains, next to
rivers and waterfalls
They are seen in bright colored bunches, right
next to the beasts
Even as the sun slips away and leaves behind a
painted sunset
Wild flowers flourish throughout all of
Yellowstone
Some even thrive right next to boiling hot,
acidic, geysers

The smell of Sulphur floats in the air, from the
hot spring and geysers
It's just one of the many unique things found in
this impressive nature

The vast land and mountains of Yellowstone
Hold many soul refreshing sites such as
powerful waterfalls
Snow in June, thick forests, open fields with
flowers, and gorgeous sunsets
Highlight the sky behind black bears other
beasts

Wolves and Coyotes are also among the park's
beasts
You can sometimes see them out past the
geysers
Once, a Blue Heron, graced us with its presence
just before the sunset
Colored the sky above the river that cut through
this bountiful nature
The Osprey nests above and the log jams below
the waterfalls
are also a few more amazing sites in
Yellowstone

It is much more than just beasts roaming in
nature
Even the geysers and rushing waterfalls
And bright sunsets are mere specks in the
grandeur of Yellowstone

Night Comes

I see a twinkle in the trees
Underneath the night sky
It moves about with ease

The warmth of the day fades
As the darkness of night grows
Hot to cool - light to dark, it trades

An owls hoots in the distance
Nearby a cricket chirps
I'm reminded of their existence

Although each day the sun must set
The night will never leave us with regret

Home

I love this farmhouse kitchen
and the hand carved table
that sits next to the window.
I can sit here and watch my mother
pick apples from our tree.
I can hear the soft wind whisper.

Many laughs, talks, and whispers
have been shared in this old kitchen.
I remember falling out of that tree
when I saw the fresh baked cookies on this table.
I always looked inside for Mother
and she always looked for me outside the
window.

Two worlds existed through the window.
One indoors with laughing, whispers,
and treats baked by Mother.
Another world was outside the kitchen
and away from the hand carved table;
one filled with adventure up in a tree.

I still come to sit and look out at the tree
through our big farmhouse window.
Scratches perfect our hand carved table

with memories of laughter and whispers.
My favorite place to be is in this kitchen
making memories with Mother.

Sweet aroma of pies baked by Mother
with the apples she picked from our tree
fills up the kitchen
and drifts out the window.
I inhale the sweet smell and whisper,
"Oh, yum", while I wait for piece at the table.

This hand carved table made from a tree
is where Mother and I sit to look out the
window.
This is home she whispers in her kitchen

Friends and Tea

Sitting Outside with a friend
We watch our children play.
Behind them sits a tabby cat
who enjoys the bright sunshine
as much as the children. Pure happiness
engulfs us as we drink our tea.

It is such a treat to have my tea
with people I love; especially my friend.
I think it brings us all some happiness;
it definitely encourages the children to play.
The best times are when there is a lot of
sunshine,
so we can count on seeing the tabby cat.

Or maybe, just seeing that tabby cat
is a simple reminder to sit down for tea.
Even if the day has no sunshine,
it's still great to just sit with a friend.
If dark skies chase us inside for play
we will undoubtedly still find some happiness.

Afterall, so many things bring about happiness -
Children laughing, long chats, even tabby cats.

There are so many different things the children play
inside or outside during our tea.
I just need to be able to sit with my friend
to feel like my day is filled with happiness.

Today, thankfully, is filled with sunshine.
It's overflowing with happiness.
I have all that i need and that is my friend,
well, and maybe that tabby cat.
Of course we'll need our tea
to sip while our children play.

As grown-ups we forget to stop and play;
even when the outside is offering bright
sunshine.
Although, we don't usually forget our tea,
so that can at least bring us some happiness.
Sometimes, I am alone with just the tabby cat,
but I can tell she thinks of me as a friend.

Sometimes i sit and watch her play just to see
her happiness.
with or without sunshine, I love that tabby cat.
So I may be sitting alone for tea, but I'll still be
with a friend.

A Place of Wonders

Yearning for places of majestic beauty, I think of
the
Environments I have seen during my travels.
Some have been
Lengthy open fields filled with wildflowers and
Little critters, such as prairie dogs, and even
larger ones, like antelope.
Often, I've seen rivers and streams meandering
along the highways, even
Waterfalls have decorated the hillsides I have
passed by.
Scenes come and go through my mind as I try to
narrow my
Thoughts down to just a few of my favorite
places. I
Once thought the giant roaring waterfalls I sat
next to in
Niagara Falls State Park were the most beautiful
things my
Eyes had ever seen. They are, indeed, an
unforgettable
Natural wonder that will live in my memories
for
A lifetime! Still, I know my soul needs to be
recharged, perhaps, among the

Timbers of a great forest I'll find refreshment.
Specks of sunlight may peak in.
Imagine the deer nibbling at leaves on low
branches at day and
Owls hooting in the cool evening air. I know that
both the day and the
Night will offer a relaxing experience. I love the
forest, but
Alas, that isn't quite what I'm yearning for. I
want more,
Like, I want all of it! Fields of wildflowers in
yellows, purples,
Pinks, and blues. Gigantic Waterfalls racing and
rushing down over cliffs,
And forests to hike filled with critters galore.
Yet, I want more! I want geysers
Reaching hundreds of feet in the air with each
burst, and mountains! I
Know exactly where I want to be... In
Yellowstone, a park with it all!!

My Everything

Multitasking all through my day,
Yelling, laughing, shrieks of joy,
Crying, whispers, pitter pats on the floor.
Hastily preparing dinner after a glance at the
clock -
Ice cream for dessert, just a
Little reprieve before my jam packed
Day nears it it's end. Another glance at the clock,
time for
Reading, then bath time and brush our teeth.
Whew,
End of the day is finally here. Before I relax it's
time for
Nighttime prayers with my littles. I
Mustn't forget to tuck them in tight with extra
hugs and kisses.
Yellow Giraffe goes right next to my blue eyed
boy. Off to sleep
Little ones, until tomorrow's light.
I am so blessed;
For each moment with them shows me they are
my
Everything!

My Grandma Said...

Be mindful of the words you say,
Especially when you are angry.
Kindness is key and kind words are
Inviting to those that hear them. They
Nudge comfort and friendship along.
Daring to use thoughtful and kind words while
Orating can bring about a peaceful and
Restorative vibe. They can set you free and
create in you a
Better person than you even knew you could be.
Exchanging kind words with one another can
Quench the fires of discord and bring about
Useful solutions that can easily be
Identified by all. The world really could become
an
Enlightened place where all the ugly
Thoughts and actions are erased.

Alone

Something is noticed on her face, all alone.
No emotion, not even a trace, all alone.

Three people leave at the same time.
But, only one can win the race, all alone.

Chasing behind, a man walks on,
the boy cannot keep the pace, all alone.

The plane takes off above us all,
Soon, it is gone without a trace, all alone.

Her life was spent helping others,
But they don't even see her face, all alone.

Holidays

We all gathered on holidays at my grandparents'
house.
Hustle and bustle were traded for happy and
calm.
Things were simple and Grandma wore her
favorite blouse.
Dinner at two and glasses of lemonade in
everyone's palm.

Hustle and bustle were traded for happy and
calm.
The frenzy is gone from preparing our potluck
dishes.
Dinner at two and glasses of lemonade in
everyone's palm.
The grown-ups give all of the kids big hugs that
squish.

The frenzy is gone from preparing our potluck
dishes.
All of the seats are full; the couch and all of the
chairs.
The grown-ups give all of the kids hugs that
squish.

Conversations in each and every room fill the
air.

All of the seats are full; the couch and all of the
chairs.
The floor is filled with kids that can't help but to
wiggle.
Conversations in each and every room fill the
air.
Some are serious, some are reminiscent, and
some are filled with giggles.

The floor is filled with kids that can't help but to
wiggle.
All of my family joined together in one place.
Some are serious, some are reminiscent, and
some are filled with giggles.
Their daily routines all interrupted and they
slowed their pace.

All of my family joined together in one place.
All worries and troubles left at the door.
Their daily routines all interrupted and they
slowed their pace.
We listened for hours as the elderly told stories
of family lore.

I miss those days, as a child, before everything
changed.

Things were simple and Grandma wore her
favorite blouse.
Back when we woke in the morning and cooked
food to exchange.
When we all gathered on holidays at my
grandparents' house.

Crab Apple Tree

As a child I often played in our crab apple tree.
That tree easily transformed minutes into hours.
As I climbed the limbs my imagination was set
free.
It became my rocket ship or my castle towers.

That tree easily transformed minutes into hours.
Each branch became a new place to play.
It became my rocket ship or my castle towers.
Sometimes it was a witch's lair or a giant
monster made of clay.

Each branch became a new place to play.
It could be a secret cave filled with spy tools.
Sometimes it was a witch's lair or giant monster
made of clay.
One thing was for sure; my imagination had no
rules!

It could be a secret cave filled with spy tools.
I'd spend a whole day up in those branches.
One thing was for sure; my imagination had no
rules!
I could set sail on a pirate ship or own several
cattle ranches.

I'd spend a whole day up in those branches.
In the Spring it's blossoms could be magical
flowers.
I could set sail on a pirate ship or own several
cattle ranches.
I often pretended the crab apples had special
powers.

In the Spring it's blossoms could be magical
flowers
that grew just for me, "the Princess of
Everyone".
I often pretended the crab apples had special
powers.
I knew when I went out to play in our tree that
the fun had just begun.

I'll never forget playing in our tree outside.
As I climbed the limbs my imagination was set
free.
So many memories, I must confide.
As a child I often played in our crab apple tree.

Battle Cry

Somewhere, deep within, I hear my battle cry.
Your cruel words no longer make my spine
shiver.
I know now that I'm a survivor, so don't you
even try.
The thought of your fist hitting me no longer
makes me quiver.

Your cruel words no longer make my spine
shiver.
Your words have no power, not your threats or
lies.
The thought of your fist hitting me no longer
makes me quiver.
I no longer cower in closets and corners,
surprise!

Your words have no power, not your threats or
lies.
My battle cry is stronger, it's much louder.
I no longer cower in closets and corners,
surprise!
I found my strength; you no longer have any
power!

My battle cry is stronger, it's much louder.
It tells me to leave, go far, far, away.
I found my strength, you no longer have any
power!
I can live without you, I'm out, I'll no longer
stay.

I tell myself to leave, go far, far away.
Leaving may have been hard, maybe even scary,
but I can live without you, I'm out, I'll no longer
stay.
Life with you was making me wary.

I'm building a new life now, where I'm safe and
at peace.
I know now that I'm a survivor, so don't you
even try.
You can't intimidate me, I've found my release.
Somewhere, deep within, I heard my battle cry.

I Watched You Grow

I watched you grow, right before my eyes.
Now you are big, no more diaper supplies.
My wee baby, now almost six feet tall.
No more holding hands at the mall.
Soon, you will leave for college, man, time flies.

Packing your clothes and books, ouch, my heart
cries.
Your infectious smile helps my heart disguise
the bittersweet feelings, so I don't stall.
I watched you grow.

Campus adventures, I cannot deny
will bring fun snd much more to your surprise.
My grown up boy will love watching football
in the stadium with his friends this fall.
Bittersweet hugs and brave goodbyes.
I watched you grow.

Silly Puppy

Silly Puppy, she loves to play.
Shenanigans the entire day.
Barking loud and chasing her tail;
running back and forth without fail.
She is too excited to just stay.

She jumps out from under the tray
and makes a mess but it's ok.
She fetches her toys from the pail.
Silly Puppy.

She chases away all of the grey.
We keep her photos on display.
Always delightful without fail;
she even tells us when there is mail.
She's funny, so we often say,
silly puppy.

Spring

Birds sing and dogs bark
Children play until it's dark
Hear the meadowlark

Soaking up the sun
A short race has just begun
They are having fun

The flowers blossom
Ivy grows up the column
Beauty, no problem

Open the windows
Saplings take root and then grow
Plow the garden rows

Alas, it's now Spring
Happiness it surely brings
Love it, everything

School

School is in session
Children carry their backpacks
Homework every night

Whiteboards not chalkboards
Learning about history
Math class is no fun

Giggling on the bus
Trading snacks from lunchboxes
School children have fun

Time to be quiet
The teacher hands out papers
Kids scribble their names

Summer is over
New classroom and new teacher
Students start to learn

Yellowstone, My Heart

Yellowstone, my heart
Tall mountains and deep valleys
Forests surround me

Wildflowers bloom
Meadows of color greet us
Rivers meander

Waterfalls astound
Huge boulders are strewn about
Awesome sights to see

Bison jam the road
Bear cubs frolic in the distance
Wolves come out at night

Hot springs all around
Steam in on the horizon
Sulfur in the air

Geysers, what a sight
Huge bursts from deep underground
Yellowstone, my heart

Butte

Butte was once my home
A town built on a mountain
What a place to roam

Mines below the ground
Abandoned, filled with water
Treasures are still found

Copper and pyrite
Rhodochrosite and moly
Malachite, azurite

Roadside veins of ore
Igneous dikes everywhere
Butte is not a bore

Protected at night
Mother Mary watches all
All is in her sight

Moose walk down the street
The snow stays all winter long
A bear, what a treat

Uptown Butte is best
Streets named after minerals
Love it, no protest